STATE GUIDES

CAPITALS

Hilarie Staton

educationalmedia.com

Introduction

The United States has 50 states. Each state has a city that is its capital. The United States has its own capital: Washington D.C. Each state government meets in that state's capital city. Most governors, the person who is in charge of the state government, live and work in the capital. The state legislature meets in the state's capital. The most important state courts usually meet in the state capital, too. This is what makes that city the capital.

Some capitals are small cities. Others are huge cities. Some capitals have a metropolitan area around them. Metropolitan areas are the towns and cities near the main city. Sometimes millions of people and businesses are in these areas.

Many people work in the capital cities. They might work for the state government or the city government. Some work for the United States government, which often has offices in a state capital. Many others work for private businesses. They work in offices, factories, or stores.

Every capital has a special building. It is called a capitol or sometimes a state house. Most are very beautiful buildings and very special to the people of that state. This is usually where at least some parts of the state government have their offices.

Remember, the city in which the government meets is called the "capital." It is spelled with an "al" at the end. The same word but spelled with an "ol" at the end, "capitol" is the building in which the government meets.

Contents

ALABAMA 4
ALASKA 5
ARIZONA 6
ARKANSAS 7
CALIFORNIA 8
COLORADO 9
CONNECTICUT 10
DELAWARE 11
FLORIDA 12
GEORGIA 13
HAWAII 14
IDAHO 15
ILLINOIS 16
INDIANA 16
IOWA 17
KANSAS 18
KENTUCKY 19
LOUISIANA 20
MAINE 21
MARYLAND 22
MASSACHUSETTS 22
MICHIGAN 23
MINNESOTA 24
MISSISSIPPI 25
MISSOURI 26
MONTANA 26

NEBRASKA 27
NEVADA 28
NEW HAMPSHIRE 29
NEW JERSEY 30
NEW MEXICO 31
NEW YORK 32
NORTH CAROLINA 32
NORTH DAKOTA 33
OHIO 34
OKLAHOMA 35
OREGON 36
PENNSYLVANIA 36
RHODE ISLAND 37
SOUTH CAROLINA 38
SOUTH DAKOTA 38
TENNESSEE 39
TEXAS 40
UTAH 41
VERMONT 42
VIRGINIA 43
WASHINGTON 44
WEST VIRGINIA 45
WISCONSIN 46
WYOMING 47
INDEX 48

Alabama

Capital: Montgomery

Montgomery is the capital of Alabama. Transportation has always been important here. American Indians used nearby paths, rivers, and streams. Later, railroads connected the city to bigger cities like New Orleans and New York. Montgomery was the first city in the Americas to have an electric streetcar system. The Wright Brothers had a flying school there, but it closed after only one student graduated.

In 1955, African Americans stopped riding the buses in Montgomery. They were protesting the unequal treatment of African Americans. For a whole year, most walked or were driven in cars. They only rode them again after the Supreme Court of the United States said that everyone on the buses had to be treated the same.

City founded:	Became Capital:	Population:	City area:
1819	1846	200,602 people (2015 estimate)	159 square miles (414 square kilometers)

Alaska

Capital: Juneau

Juneau is the capital of Alaska. The city was named for a miner who discovered gold there. Forest and steep mountains surround the city right up to the water. It is an important port because it does not get covered in ice in winter. It does not have to close like other ports in Alaska.

Juneau is on a narrow strip of Alaska's mainland. There are islands between it and the Pacific Ocean. In 1970, Juneau and Douglas Island joined together. Now, Juneau covers the largest area of any city in the United States. Also, it is the only capital to border a foreign country: Canada.

City founded:	Became Capital:	Population:	City area:
1880	Territorial Capital 1906; State Capital 1959	32,756 people (2015 estimate)	2,702 square miles (6,998 square kilometers)

Arizona

Capital: Phoenix

Phoenix is the capital of Arizona. Thousands of people have moved to Phoenix since the 1970s. The city also grew by joining with nearby communities. Today, it has more people than any other state capital. Unlike older capitals, it is very spread out with many centers. The region used to have many ranches and farms. Today most people have jobs that help other people or build things, such as electronic equipment.

Phoenix is in the hot, dry Sonoran Desert. The city depends on the water found below the ground or in the Colorado River. The faster the city grows, the more water it needs.

City founded:	Became Capital:	Population:	City area:
1868	Territorial Capital 1889; State Capital 1912	1,563,025 people (2015 estimate)	517 square miles (1,339 square kilometers)

Arkansas

Capital: Little Rock

Little Rock is the capital of Arkansas. It was an important trade center for farmers. Goods traveled from Little Rock down the Arkansas River to the Mississippi River. Today, goods also move along Little Rock's major highways. This has helped make Little Rock the largest city in Arkansas.

Bill Clinton was Governor of Arkansas and then President of the United States. A special library was built in Little Rock. The William J. Clinton Presidential Center tells about his life and his time as president.

City founded:	Became Capital:	Population:	City area:
1820	Territorial Capital 1820; State Capital 1836	197,992 people (2015 estimate)	119 square miles (308 square kilometers)

California

Capital: Sacramento

Sacramento is the capital of California. The California Gold Rush started nearby. In 1849, people walked or rode wagons across the country. They were headed to Sacramento and the goldfields. Soon a steamboat went from Sacramento to San Francisco. Then, in 1869, the new railroad crossed the country and ended in Sacramento. Now it has a harbor which connects to San Francisco Harbor. It is still at the center of a rich farming region.

When California became a state in 1850, Sacramento was not the capital. Between 1849 and 1854, California's capital moved six times. Finally, Sacramento became the permanent capital, even though other cities have wanted to be the capital.

City founded:	Became Capital:	Population:	City area:
1848	State Capital 1854	490,712 people (2015 estimate)	98 square miles (254 square kilometers)

Colorado

Capital: Denver

Denver is the capital of Colorado. Beginning in 1870, streetcars went from the city to nearby empty land. People built homes along the streetcar lines. They rode the streetcars into the city for work. Some towns became part of Denver, while others decided to stay separate. This has created a large metropolitan area.

Denver's nickname is "The Mile High City." In 1909, the city carved "One Mile Above Sea Level" into the fifteenth step of the state capitol. They had to change it because of better measuring. In 1969, they marked the eighteenth step. In 2003, they moved it again—to the thirteenth step!

City founded:	Became Capital:	Population:	City area:
1858	Territorial Capital 1867; State Capital 1876	682,545 people (2015 estimate)	153 square miles (396 square kilometers)

Connecticut

Capital: Hartford

Since colonial times, Hartford has been an important business and manufacturing center because it is on the Connecticut River. It is the capital of Connecticut. For many years, Connecticut had two capitals: Hartford and New Haven. Each had its own capitol building. In 1875, Hartford became the state's only capital. They built a new, larger capitol there.

Hartford's nickname is "The Insurance Capital of the World." In 1810, Hartford's first insurance company had its own fire department. Today many people in Hartford work for insurance companies.

City founded:	Became Capital:	Population:	City area:
1635	Shared Colonial Capital 1701; Shared State Capital 1789, State Capital 1875	124,006 people (2015 estimate)	17 square miles (44 square kilometers)

Delaware

Capital: Dover

Dover is the capital of Delaware. This small city is in a very small state. Most people in Delaware live and work in the north, around Wilmington. This is only an hour away from Dover. Many of those who live in Dover work for the state government. Delaware is so small, the state government does many things done by local governments in other states. For example, the bus system covers the whole state, not just one city.

Delaware moved its capital to Dover during the American Revolution. They thought it would be harder for the British Army to attack Dover than the old capital, New Castle.

City founded:	Became Capital:	Population:	City area:
1683	Colonial Capital 1777 State Capital 1789	37,522 people (2015 estimate)	23 square miles (60 square kilometers)

Florida

Capital: Tallahassee

Tallahassee is the capital of Florida. Spanish Florida had two parts. Each had its own capital. When Florida became part of the United States, Florida replaced its two capitals with Tallahassee which is halfway between them. Florida has talked about moving its capital closer to where most people live, but they have not moved it.

In 1978, Florida opened a new capitol. In the old one, they found over 100 pounds of stained glass in the walls. They put the pieces together to make a beautiful dome that was originally designed in 1902.

City founded:	Became Capital:	Population:	City area:
1821	Territorial Capital 1824; State Capital 1845	189,907 people (2015 estimate)	100 square miles (259 square kilometers)

 # Georgia

Capital: Atlanta

Atlanta is the capital of Georgia. It has over five million people living in its metropolitan area. That's more than any other state capital. The area has many businesses, offices, and factories. The state government does not have the most workers in the city. In fact, some state offices have moved to other cities in Georgia.

Transportation has been important to Atlanta's growth. In 1837, they began building a town to be the end of a new railroad. Its name was soon changed to Atlanta. Atlanta's railroads were important during the Civil War and for rebuilding after the war. Today the Atlanta airport is one of the world's busiest airports.

City founded:	Became Capital:	Population:	City area:
1837	State Capital 1868	463,878 people (2015 estimate)	133 square miles (84 square kilometers)

Hawaii

Capital: Honolulu

Honolulu is the capital of Hawaii. Honolulu is very important to the United States military and very popular with tourists. People from many places live in Hawaii. The original settlers were from other Pacific Islands. Around half of Honolulu's people are from Asian countries, like Japan, China, or the Philippines.

Honolulu is on the island of Oahu. It has the longest borders of any city. Several islets, or small islands, are also part of the city. The city's border is measured by going around every one.

City founded:	Became Capital:	Population:	City area:
1820	Hawaiian Kingdom Capital 1850 Territorial Capital 1906; State Capital 1959	32,756 people (2015 estimate)	2,702 square miles (6,998 square kilometers)

 # Idaho

Capital: Boise

Boise is the capital of Idaho. Boise started as a fort and town for fur traders and gold miners. Even after it became the capital, it remained a small town. Today it is still important to the farms and ranches in the northern Rocky Mountains.

At first, getting to Boise was not easy. It was a long way from other cities. Thousands of people came through the area on wagon trains headed west. For many years, wagon trains were the only way supplies reached Boise. Because of the nearby steep land, passenger trains did not arrive there until 1925.

City founded:	Became Capital:	Population:	City area:
1864	Territorial Capital 1864; State Capital 1890	218,281 people (2015 estimate)	79 square miles (205 square kilometers)

Illinois

Capital: Springfield

Springfield is the capital of Illinois. In 1837 Abraham Lincoln voted to move the capital to Springfield. He gave many speeches here. Today, much of the area around Springfield remains farmland.

Although Springfield is the capital, many of the state's top elected officials work out of offices in Chicago. Chicago is Illinois' biggest city but not its capital. Springfield is about 200 miles (322 kilometers) from Chicago.

City founded:	Became Capital:	Population:	City area:
1820	State Capital 1837	116,565 people (2015 estimate)	60 square miles (155 square kilometers)

Indiana

Capital: Indianapolis

Indianapolis is the capital of Indiana. It is the fourth largest state capital in population. It is one of the world's biggest cities that is not on water used for transportation, like a river, ocean, or lake.

(Indiana continued)

In 1909, the Indianapolis Motor Speedway opened so automobile factories could test their cars. Since 1911, a famous auto race, the Indianapolis 500, has been held there.

City founded:	Became Capital:	Population:	City area:
1821	1821	853,173 people (2015 estimate)	361 square miles (935 square kilometers)

 # Iowa

Capital: Des Moines

Des Moines is the capital of Iowa. The government moved the capital to Des Moines so that it would be closer to the center of the state. It became an important business center, especially for government offices and insurance companies.

Des Moines was founded near where the Des Moines River meets the Raccoon River.

City founded:	Became Capital:	Population:	City area:
1845	State Capital 1857	210,330 people (2015 estimate)	81 square miles (210 square kilometers)

Kansas

Capital: Topeka

Topeka is the capital of Kansas. It is in the region where most of Kansas's people live and where most of its businesses are. The rest of the state is much more rural, with farms and small towns. In 1966, a disastrous tornado destroyed or damaged almost 4,000 homes in Topeka.

The Kansas State Capitol took 37 years to build. It was finally finished in 1903. By law, the Kansas state legislature can meet for as long as it wants in odd-numbered years. In even-numbered years it cannot meet for more than ninety days.

City founded:	Became Capital:	Population:	City area:
1854	State Capital 1861	127,265 people (2015 estimate)	60 square miles (155 square kilometers)

Kentucky

Capital: Frankfort

Frankfort is the capital of Kentucky. It is on a double bend in the Kentucky River. Some parts of the city are across the river from other parts. The "new" Kentucky State Capitol was built on the opposite side of the river from the "old" capitol. It is the fourth capitol and was completed in 1910. The first two burned down. The third one became too small for the growing state government. The home of the Kentucky Historical Society is now in the "old" capitol.

Frankfort is a small city, but is between the larger nearby cities of Lexington and Louisville.

City founded:	Became Capital:	Population	City area:
1786	State Capital 1792	27,830 people (2015 estimate)	14 square miles (36 square kilometers)

Louisiana

Capital: Baton Rouge

Baton Rouge is the capital of Louisiana. River barges travel down the Mississippi River to this port city. Ships from the ocean travel up the Mississippi to this port.

The H.P. Long Bridge crosses the Mississippi River in Baton Rouge. Most ships have to unload their cargo in Baton Rouge because the bridge is too low for them to go under it.

The Louisiana State Capitol was finished in 1932. It is 34 stories tall. This makes it the tallest state capitol in the United States.

City founded:	Became Capital:	Population:	City area:
1719	State Capital 1846	228,590 people (2015 estimate)	77 square miles (199 square kilometers)

Maine

Capital: Augusta

Augusta is the capital of Maine. During the colonial period, traders arrived in the area. A town was built on the Kennebec River. The town split into two until 1797 when they joined together again as Augusta. It is the third smallest capital city in the United States. About forty percent of the workers in Augusta work for the state government.

The Maine State House was finished in 1832. It has been made bigger, and is still used by Maine's governor and legislature.

City founded:	Became Capital:	Population:	City area:
1797	State Capital 1827	18,471 people (2015 estimate)	55 square miles (142 square kilometers)

Maryland

Capital: Annapolis

Annapolis is the capital of Maryland. In 1783 and 1784 Annapolis was also the capital of the United States. The Continental Congress met here to sign the treaty that ended the American Revolution.

Many people around Annapolis work for The United States government. Some work at the United States Naval Academy. Many more work in government offices at Fort George G. Meade.

City founded:	Became Capital:	Population:	City area:
1649	Colonial Capital 1694 State Capital 1777 U.S. Capital 1789	39,474 people (2015 estimate)	7 square miles (18 square kilometers)

Massachusetts

Capital: Boston

Boston is the capital of Massachusetts. The city has more people living in it per square mile, almost 12,800, than any other state capital. This makes it a busy and crowded place. Many businesses in the city deal with money, such as banks.

(Massachusetts continued)

Boston is in one of the largest Metropolitan Statistical Areas in the United States. Four and a half million people live in this area.

City founded:	Became Capital:	Population:	City area:
1630	Colonial Capital 1632; State Capital 1789	667,137 people (2015 estimate)	48 square miles (124 square kilometers)

Michigan

Capital: Lansing

Lansing is the capital of Michigan. The capital was moved here from Detroit in 1847. People were afraid that the British in Canada would capture Detroit like they did during the War of 1812. For a long time, many people in Lansing worked in automobile factories. Today, more people work for the state government.

In 1836, two brothers returned to their home in Lansing, New York, after visiting Michigan. They sold the land they had purchased in Michigan to people in New York. When these people arrived in the new town, called Biddle City, they found no city at all. Most of the land was under water! They stayed anyway and built a new town. They renamed the town after the village they'd left in New York: Lansing.

City founded:	Became Capital:	Population:	City area:
1836	State Capital 1847	114,299 people (2015 estimate)	36 square miles (93 square kilometers)

Minnesota

Capital: St. Paul

St. Paul is the capital of Minnesota. It is alongside Minneapolis. Together they are called the Twin Cities. St. Paul has more shoreline along the Mississippi River than any other city. It is on the first part of the Mississippi River where it is deep enough to be used for transportation. Goods also came and went on railroads. These connected St. Paul to both the West Coast and the East Coast.

The first town in this spot was known as "Pig's Eye Landing." This was changed to St. Paul in 1849. The territory's legislature met there in a log hotel.

City founded:	Became Capital:	Population:	City area:
1838	Territorial Capital 1849; State Capital 1858	300,851 people (2015 estimate)	52 square miles (135 square kilometers)

Mississippi

Capital: Jackson

Jackson is the capital of Mississippi. The city was founded in 1821 so the capital would be in the center of the state. By the next year, a capitol had been built and the legislature was meeting there. However, it grew slowly because the city was in the wilderness.

The city was named for General Andrew Jackson, who became president of the United States in 1829. In 1903, a new capitol building was finished. The back taxes owed by the Illinois Central Railroad paid for it. The old Mississippi Capitol became a museum.

City founded:	Became Capital:	Population:	City area:
1821	State Capital 1821	170,674 people (2015 estimate)	111 square miles (287 square kilometers)

Missouri

Capital: Jefferson City

Jefferson City is the capital of Missouri. When the Missouri state legislature wanted a new capital, they hired Daniel Morgan Boone, the son of Daniel Boone. He laid out the new city in 1821. It was named for President Thomas Jefferson.

Thomas Hart Benton visited people all over Missouri while he was painting his huge mural, or wall painting, in the state capitol. He finished it in 1936. He included his family, outlaws, fishing parties, and even historical scenes of slavery.

City founded:	Became Capital:	Population:	City area:
1821	State Capital 1821	43,169 people (2015 estimate)	36 square miles (93 square kilometers)

Montana

Capital: Helena

Helena is the capital of Montana. In 1864, gold was discovered in Last Chance Gulch. Today the gulch is Helena's Main Street. It has a walking mall with shops and restaurants.

(Montana continued)

The statue on top of the capitol used to be called "Liberty" but no one knew what its real name was or who made it. In 2006, the granddaughter of the man who made it contacted the State Historical Society. They found out he called it "Montana" not "Liberty."

City founded:	Became Capital:	Population:	City area:
1864	Territorial Capital 1875; State Capital 1889	30,581 people (2015 estimate)	16 square miles (41 square kilometers)

 # Nebraska

Capital: Lincoln

Lincoln is the capital of Nebraska. The first settlers built homes here because they found salt nearby. They named the town Lancaster. When the town was chosen as the state capital, the name was changed to honor President Abraham Lincoln.

In 1937 Nebraska changed its government. Its legislature only has one house. This is different than any other state or the United States.

The tall Nebraska Capitol was finished in 1932. It was the first state capitol to be in the modern style of a skyscraper.

City founded:	Became Capital:	Population:	City area:
1856	State Capital 1867	277,348 people (2015 estimate)	89 square miles (231 square kilometers)

Nevada

Capital: Carson City

Carson City is the capital of Nevada. Its name is from the nearby Carson River. The river was named for Kit Carson. At first mining, ranching, and transportation were important to the city. Today, most people in Carson City work for the city, state, or United States government. Nevada's Governor still has offices in the original Nevada State Capitol. The legislature and Supreme Court meet in nearby buildings.

Carson City borders Lake Tahoe, so does California. Carson City is one of only two capitals on the border of two states.

City founded:	Became Capital:	Population	City area:
1858	Territorial Capital 1861; State Capital 1864	54,521 people (2015 estimate)	145 square miles (376 square kilometers)

New Hampshire

Capital: Concord

Concord is the capital of New Hampshire. The New Hampshire State House was built in 1819. Although the capitol was made larger, the legislature still meets in its original rooms. When the capitol was built, they put a wooden eagle on its dome. It was painted gold. The eagle was finally taken down because the weather was destroying it. It was replaced with a metal one covered in gold.

City founded:	Became Capital:	Population:	City area:
1727	State Capital 1808	46,620 people (2015 estimate)	665 square miles (1,722 square kilometers)

New Jersey

Capital: Trenton

Trenton is the capital of New Jersey. On July 8, 1776, one of the first three readings of the Declaration of Independence was here. During the American Revolution, George Washington brought his army across the frozen Delaware River from Pennsylvania into New Jersey. They surprised the British who had captured Trenton. This was an important victory for the American Army.

Trenton borders the state of Pennsylvania. It is the second oldest capital in the United States. The United States Congress met in Trenton in 1784.

City founded:	Became Capital:	Population:	City area:
1679	US Capital 1784; State Capital 1789	84,225 people (2015 estimate)	8 square miles (21 square kilometers)

New Mexico

Capital: Santa Fe

Santa Fe is the capital of New Mexico. It is the oldest capital in the United States. It was the capital under two foreign countries: Spain and Mexico. Today, many artists, especially from local American Indian cultures, make Santa Fe an important creative city. It has a huge Indian Market and a Folk Art Market. They feature many different handmade items.

The first capitol, The Palace of the Governors, was built in 1610. A new capitol, called The Roundhouse, was built in 1966. It is the only capitol that is round.

City founded:	Became Capital:	Population:	City area:
1610	Spanish Colonial Capital 1610; Mexican Provincial Capital 1821; US Territorial Capital 1851; State Capital 1912	84,09 people (2015 estimate)	46 square miles (119 square kilometers)

New York

Capital: Albany

Albany is the capital of New York. Dutch colonial traders founded Albany along the Hudson River. Over the years, goods moved in and out of Albany on the river, the Erie Canal, the railroads, ocean-going ships, and interstate highways.

The capitol, finished in 1899, is still in use. It is part of Empire State Plaza. In order to build this plaza, thousands of people and businesses had to move. Eleven new buildings went up, including the 44-floor Corning Tower. It is the tallest building in the state outside of New York City. Thousands of people who work for New York State have their offices in the buildings at the Empire State Plaza.

City founded:	Became Capital:	Population:	City area:
1624	State Capital 1797	98,469 people (2015 estimate)	21 square miles (54 square kilometers)

North Carolina

Capital: Raleigh

Raleigh is the capital of North Carolina. In 1792, the state bought land to develop a capital city in central North Carolina. They named the city Raleigh after the explorer Sir Walter Raleigh.

(North Carolina continued)

It was built on a main route across North Carolina. Today, Raleigh and two neighboring cities are called the Research Triangle. The colleges, businesses, hospitals, and government offices in this area employ many workers. Many are developing new goods and services that people all over the world will use.

City founded:	Became Capital:	Population:	City area:
1792	State Capital 1792	451,066 people (2015 estimate)	143 square miles (370 square kilometers)

 # North Dakota

Capital: Bismarck

Bismarck is the capital of North Dakota. When Bismarck became the capital, it grew quickly. Some people settled there because the railroad was being built nearby. Others came to open stores for the miners looking for gold in the Black Hills.

When North Dakota's first capitol caught fire in 1930, Bismarck only had three firemen. Although other people joined them to try and save the capitol, it was destroyed.

City founded:	Became Capital:	Population:	City area:
1872	Territorial Capital 1882 State Capital 1889	71,167 people (2015 estimate)	31 square miles (80 square kilometers)

Ohio

Capital: Columbus

Columbus was founded as Ohio's capital. It is in the center of the state and near transportation, like rivers, railroads, and highways. Like many Ohio cities, Columbus once had many factories where most people worked. Today, more people in Columbus work in offices, either for the government or for private businesses.

Since 1950, the size of Columbus has changed. It grew by annexing, or taking over, the places around it. It grew from 40 square miles (104 square kilometers) to 217 square miles (562 square kilometers).

City founded:	Became Capital:	Population:	City area:
1812	State Capital 1812	850,106 people (2015 estimate)	217 square miles (562 square kilometers)

Oklahoma

Capital: Oklahoma City

Oklahoma City is the capital of Oklahoma. Oklahoma was part of Indian Territory, until the western half became the Oklahoma Territory. The area went from empty land to a city of 10,000 in one day. This 1889 land rush created a city of tents. This grew into Oklahoma City. Once the railroads came through, business and industry grew quickly.

In 1928, oil was discovered under the city. It became the largest oil strike ever made. Oklahoma is the only state with working oil wells around its capitol. One oil well is in a flowerbed and called Petunia #1.

City founded:	Became Capital:	Population:	City area:
1889	State Capital 1910	631,346 people (2015 estimate)	606 square miles (1,570 square kilometers)

Oregon

Capital: Salem

Salem is the capital of Oregon. From 1851 until 1864 when voters made a final decision, Oregon kept changing its capital city. Salem is in an agricultural and forest area. Many of its factories process food or make paper and wood products.

The first capitol was only two years old when it burned down in 1855. After that, for about twenty years, the Oregon Legislature met in rented rooms. A new capitol was finished in 1876.

City founded:	Became Capital:	Population:	City area:
1848	Territorial 1851 and 1855 State Capital 1864	164,549 people (2015 estimate)	48 square miles (124 square kilometers)

Pennsylvania

Capital: Harrisburg

Harrisburg is the capital of Pennsylvania. It was built far inland from important colonial cities but on important transportation routes. People have traveled to and through Harrisburg on stagecoaches, canals, railroads, and in cars and trucks.

(Pennsylvania continued)

When the Pennsylvania capitol burned in 1897, it was snowing. The Pennsylvania legislature had to move to a nearby church. After that, some people wanted to move the capital back to Philadelphia, but they built a new capitol in Harrisburg instead.

City founded:	Became Capital:	Population:	City area:
1785	State Capital 1812	49,081 people (2015 estimate)	8 square miles (21 square kilometers)

 # Rhode Island

Capital: Providence

Providence is the capital of Rhode Island. Rhode Island is the smallest state in size. Most of its people live within fifteen miles (24 kilometers) of Providence. This seaport was an important trading and manufacturing center.

Rhode Island's State House is special. There are only three other buildings in the world that have an unsupported marble dome bigger than Rhode Island's.

Before the Declaration of Independence, Rhode Island passed its own Independence Act. However, it was the last state to ratify, or approve, the Constitution.

City founded:	Became Capital:	Population:	City area:
1636	State Capital 1900	179,207 people (2015 estimate)	18 square miles (47 square kilometers)

South Carolina

Capital: Columbia

Columbia is the capital of South Carolina. In 1786, Columbia was built to be the capital. Although it was a planned city with wide streets, the streets were not paved until 1908. Today, it is the largest city in South Carolina.

The small farmers in the west and the plantation owners in the east both wanted the capital near them. Instead the state legislature built a new town, Columbia, in the middle of the state to be the capital.

City founded:	Became Capital:	Population:	City area:
1786	State Capital 1786	133,803 people (2015 estimate)	132 square miles (342 square kilometers)

South Dakota

Capital: Pierre

Pierre is the capital of South Dakota. It has the second smallest population of any state capital. It is 105 miles (169 kilometers) from the closest city, Huron. It is only two miles (3 kilometers) from the geographical center of the whole United States.

(South Dakota continued)

Voters approved Pierre as their capital in three different elections. After that, they built the capitol. Today, those elected to South Dakota's legislature do not have an office in the capitol. Most work from their homes or businesses.

City founded:	Became Capital:	Population	City area:
1880	State Capital 1890	14,000 people (2015 estimate)	13 square miles (34 square kilometers)

Tennessee

Capital: Nashville

Nashville is the capital of Tennessee. It has developed into a business center with many different types of businesses. These include healthcare and printing, but it is known for its music business. People come to Nashville to listen to music or break into the music business. Nashville is also home to several important colleges.

In 1963, the Nashville city government and Davidson County governments joined together into one government.

City founded:	Became Capital:	Population:	City area:
1806	State Capital 1843	654,610 people (2015 estimate)	475 square miles (1,230 square kilometers)

Texas

Capital: Austin

Austin is the capital of Texas. Some people opposed Austin becoming the capital because it was so far from where most Texans lived. However, today it is home to many computer and healthcare businesses. Many people work for local colleges or the state and local governments.

During the Texas Republic, Austin fought with bigger Texas cities, like Houston, about which would be the capital. The government moved away from Austin in 1842, but many important papers stayed in Austin until it became the capital again in 1846.

City founded:	Became Capital:	Population:	City area:
1839	Republic of Texas 1839; State Capital 1846	931,830 people (2015 estimate)	298 square miles (772 square kilometers)

Utah

Capital: Salt Lake City

Salt Lake City is the capital of Utah. A group of Mormons founded the city along the Great Salt Lake. Mining and railroads helped build the city into a trade and transportation center for the area. After Utah became a state, it was 20 years before they finished the Utah Capitol.

Today the Church of Jesus Christ of Latter-day Saints (Mormons) has their headquarters in Salt Lake City. There is also a world famous center for learning about a family's past history. Many people have found out the names of those who were in their family a hundred or more years ago.

City founded:	Became Capital:	Population:	City area:
1847	Territorial Capital 1856; State Capital 1896	192,672 people (2015 estimate)	111 square miles (287 square kilometers)

Vermont

Capital: Montpelier

Montpelier is the capital of Vermont. It has the smallest population of any state capital. The last count showed that the city's population is getting smaller, not larger. More people in Montpelier work for the State of Vermont than any other type of business.

For 14 years, Vermont had no capital and the legislature met in different towns. Then, in 1805, Montpelier was chosen as the capital. In 1857, the Vermont Capitol burned. People in Montpelier saved many books, paintings, and important papers from the fire. They also paid to rebuild the capitol after the fire.

City founded:	Became Capital:	Population:	City area:
1787	State Capital 1805	7,592 people (2015 estimate)	11 square miles (28 square kilometers)

Virginia

Capital: Richmond

Richmond is the capital of Virginia. The British Army chased the Virginia State Government out of Richmond twice during the American Revolution. During the Civil War, it was the capital of the Confederacy. Today, many people in Richmond work for private companies like banks, stores, and factories.

Thomas Jefferson had strong ideas about what the Virginia State Capitol should look like. While he was in France, Jefferson worked with people there to make a model of his design. He sent it to Richmond. It took 15 years to build the capitol. That model is still on display inside the capitol.

City founded:	Became Capital:	Population:	City area:
1737	State Capital 1780	220,289 people (2015 estimate)	60 square miles (155 square kilometers)

Washington

Capital: Olympia

Olympia is the capital of Washington. When it was founded, a few trails led to it through dense forests. Steamboats, called the Mosquito Fleet, traveled Puget Sound to reach Olympia's harbor. They brought people, mail, even fish and eggs to Olympia.

Several earthquakes have rocked Olympia. The 1949 earthquake damaged eight buildings near the capitol. The center of the 2001 earthquake was only 10 miles away from the city. The state capitol has been improved so it can withstand future earthquakes.

City founded:	Became Capital:	Population:	City area:
1851	Territorial Capital 1853 State Capital 1889	50,302 people (2015 estimate)	17 square miles (44 square kilometers)

West Virginia

Capital: Charleston

Charleston is the capital of West Virginia. West Virginia was part of Virginia until the Civil War. It became a separate state after its voters, the United States Congress, and President Lincoln all agreed. The state capital moved back and forth between Wheeling and Charleston until 1885. In 1921, the state capitol burned. The new one was so quickly built that it was called the "pasteboard capitol." The present capitol was finally completed in 1932.

At first, Charleston had a big salt industry. Nearby factories made the barrels and flatboats to move the salt. Steamboats arrived on the river. Roads linked Charleston to other Virginia towns.

City founded:	Became Capital:	Population:	City area:
1794	State Capital 1870 and 1885	49,736 people (2015 estimate)	32 square miles (83 square kilometers)

Wisconsin

Capital: Madison

Madison is the capital of Wisconsin. It has many farms nearby. Their crops are shipped all over the United States. The University of Wisconsin-Madison is an important part of the city. Many people work for the university or run businesses for its students.

Madison was named the capital before the town was built. Nothing was built for another year and it remained a small town until about 1854. Once the railroad arrived many factories sent farm equipment and farm products to the rest of the country.

City founded:	Became Capital:	Population:	City area:
1837	Territorial Capital 1836 State Capital 1848	248,951 people (2015 estimate)	77 square miles (199 square kilometers)

Wyoming

Capital: Cheyenne

Cheyenne is the capital of Wyoming. It was founded as a supply town for the railroad being built across the United States. It was called "The City of Tents." Then the name was changed to Cheyenne to honor the American Indians that lived nearby.

Railroads started Cheyenne, but it grew for other reasons, too. Soon, many large cattle and sheep ranches were in the area. The soldiers from nearby army forts often came to town. Miners bought their supplies in Cheyenne before they headed out to search for gold in the Black Hills.

City founded:	Became Capital:	Population:	City area:
1867	Territorial Capital 1869 State Capital 1890	63,335 people (2015 estimate)	24.52 square miles (65 square kilometers)

 # Index

Alabama 4	Louisiana 20	Ohio 34
Alaska 5	Maine 21	Oklahoma 35
Arizona 6	Maryland 22	Oregon 36
Arkansas 7	Massachusetts 22	Pennsylvania 36
California 8	Michigan 23	Rhode Island 37
Colorado 9	Minnesota 24	South Carolina 38
Connecticut 10	Mississippi 25	South Dakota 38
Delaware 11	Missouri 26	Tennessee 39
Florida 12	Montana 26	Texas 40
Georgia 13	Nebraska 27	Utah 41
Hawaii 14	Nevada 28	Vermont 42
Idaho 15	New Hampshire 29	Virginia 43
Illinois 16	New Jersey 30	Washington 44
Indiana 16	New Mexico 31	West Virginia 45
Iowa 17	New York 32	Wisconsin 46
Kansas 18	North Carolina 32	Wyoming 47
Kentucky 19	North Dakota 33	

© 2018 Rourke Educational Media

All rights reserved. No part of this book may be reproduced or utilized in any form or by any means, electronic or mechanical including photocopying, recording, or by any information storage and retrieval system without permission in writing from the publisher.

www.rourkeeducationalmedia.com

PHOTO CREDITS: Cover:Main photo, Georgia Capital © ESB Professional, Alabama © Sean Pavone, Delaware © Nagel Photography, New Mexico © Sherry Talbot, Ohio © Joseph Sohm, Tennessee © f11photo;
Inside: Alaska © Pauk; Alabama © Sean Pavone; Arkansas, Arizona, Delaware, Pennsylvania, South Dakota © Nagel Photography; California © Mark R; Colorado © Moonborne; Connecticut © jiawangkun; Georgia © ESB Professional; Florida © JSvideos; Hawaii © Theodore Trimmer; Idaho © Frank L Junior; Illinois © RRuntsch; Indiana © photo.ua; Iowa © Christopher Boswell; Kansas, Missouri, © Gino Santa Maria; Kentucky © Alexey Stiop; Louisiana © Beyza-Veysel; Maine, New York © Felix Lipov; Maryland © Paul Brady Photography; Massachusetts © Byelikova Oksana; Michigan © Jason Grindle; Minnesota © Scruggelgreen; Mississippi © Sean Pavone; Montana © Christopher Boswell; Nebraska © Steven Frame; Nevada © Joseph Sohm; New Hampshire © Zack Frank; New Jersey © Aneese; New Mexico © Sherry Talbot; North carolina © ESB Professional; North Dakota © Ace Diamond, Ohio © Joseph Sohm; Oklahoma © W. Scott McGill, Oregon © Rigucci, Rhode Island © Thomas Barrat, South Carolina © meunierd, Tennessee © f11photo, Texas © clayton harrison, Utah © Carlo Emanuele Barbi, Vermont © Steven Frame, Virginia © vincent noel, Washington © Nadia Borisevich, West Virginia © ABEMOS, Wisconsin © UmFOTO, Wyoming © Jonathan Lenz

Edited by: Keli Sipperley   Cover and Interior design by: Nicola Stratford   www.nicolastratford.com

Library of Congress PCN Data

CAPITALS / Hilarie Staton
 (STATE GUIDES)
  ISBN 978-1-68342-404-8 (hard cover)
  ISBN 978-1-68342-474-1 (soft cover)
  ISBN 978-1-68342-570-0 (e-Book)
Library of Congress Control Number: 2017931410

Rourke Educational Media
Printed in the United States of America, North Mankato, Minnesota

RECEIVED JAN 1 5 2019